TABLE OF CONTENTS

Foreword

Affirmations, truly, are simple. They are *you* being in conscious command of your thoughts. They are brief, mighty statements. If you say them or think them or even hear them, they get to be the thoughts that produce your reality. Affirmations, then, are your conscious thoughts. Get all the info you need here.

THE POWER OF AFFIRMATIONS

How to attract your ideal life through affirmations

CHAPTER I

Introduction

Synopsis

Research has demonstrated that we have between 45,000 and 51,000 thoughts a day. That's about 150 to 300 thoughts a moment. Research has likewise demonstrated that for most individuals 80% of those thoughts are damaging.

The Basics

Now, we have been taught to think that many of these 51,000 thoughts are "sub-conscious" thoughts meaning that they're below our conscious cognizance level. Affirmations make your sub-conscious thoughts conscious.

Affirmations make you consciously cognizant of your thoughts. If you begin making conscious favorable thoughts, you become more aware of the damaging thoughts that are constantly threatening to take over.

It's an interesting phenomenon, in truth. It proves true what your mother always cautioned: be careful of what you think as what you think is what you get. She was essentially telling you that you produce what you think about.

When you're not cognizant of your thoughts, they tend to be damaging. And not being aware of your thoughts tends to induce an awful spiral downward.

Remember that 80% figure of damaging thoughts? It gets worse. Whatever you're thinking about, 90% gets carried forward to the next day's 51,000 thoughts.

So, if you're thinking damaging thoughts, you'll cause yourself to think more damaging thoughts. This is not going to get you out ofyour mess.

Affirmations may change all of that! Affirmations make you conscious of your thoughts. To affirm means to state something positively. It means to announce firmly and assert something to be true. Affirmations are statements where you assert that what you wish to be real is real.

Here are a few affirmations you can use:

- I'm a success in all that I do
- I feel pleased, I feel healthy, I feel fantastic
- Everything feels just so correct
- I'm a money mogul
- My mind is clear centered and energized

Over time they overwrite any limiting or damaging beliefs you might have about yourself or about not being able to do something and substitute them with favorable thoughts and beliefs which instill self-confidence, belief, positivity, ambitiousness and much more.

Somebody who is perhaps a bit shy or un-confident would repeat affirmations about being confident. They would want to change themselves from being timid and introverted to becoming self- assured and more outgoing perhaps, and so they'd utilize favorable affirmations and repeat them again and again. And eventually they'd begin to sink in - the repetitive, favorable self-talk would begin to become a self-fulfilling prophecy. You can use the power of positive repetition for yourself!

Utilizing favorable affirmations gives you back command of your mind and the information it gets. It puts you in the driver's seat of your brain and lets you flood it with favorable information which will change you for the better!

CHAPTER II

Intro To Affirmative Prayer

Synopsis

Affirmative prayer is a sort of prayer or a metaphysical process that's centered on a favorable outcome instead of a negative situation. For instance, an individual who is experiencing some form of illness would focus the prayer on the wanted state of perfect health and affirm this desired intention "as if already occurred" instead of identifying the illness and then asking The Higher Power for help to do away with it.

About Prayer

William James described affirmative prayer as a component of the American metaphysical healing movement that he called the "mind- cure"; he depicted it as America's "only decidedly original contribution to the systemic philosophy of life.

What sets affirmative prayer apart from secular affirmations of the autosuggestion sort taught in previous times, is that affirmative prayer addresses the practitioner to The Higher Power, the Divine, the Creative Mind, accentuating the seemingly practical aspects of religion.

A few members of the self-help and self-improvement movements advocate affirmative prayer in addition to or rather than secular affirmations. The choice is for the most part an individual one, based on the beliefs of the person.

Five Steps of Affirmative Prayer

1. Acknowledgement: Remind yourself of the nature of life/The Higher Power/spirit. This is the chief ingredient in affirmative prayer: acknowledgement. Your moldiness knows what the nature of The Higher Power is before going further. If, for instance, you used to believe that The Higher Power was an angry, vengeful Higher Power, now is the time to remind yourself of the bigger truth. Remind yourself of the lawful and loving nature of The Higher Power.

2. Uniting: Remind yourself that you come from life/spirit/The Higher Power. If The Higher Power exists and is everything good and fantastic, but you're on the outside looking in, why even bother to pray? Remind yourself that The Higher Power is the source and Creator of everything, including you, including your wants. This is a different crucial ingredient in affirmative prayer.

3. Actualization: understand life already is the thing or experience you want. If you can want it, imagine it, picture it, it must exist in the brain. Otherwise, where did you get the thought? Remember, the beginning premise of this is, there exists a central Unity. There's no place other than brain to get your idea. For an effective prayer, you want to continue contemplating that you deservehappiness", that's when the realization comes. When you open your eyes, your desire might not be sitting on the floor in front of you, but don't be duped... Your brain is already at work making it happen.

If doubts come up... Don't simply ignore. Face them! Speak the truth about what you're fearing will or won't happen...for instance, if you feel that you might never afford a new automobile, you could say, "I have this desire and along with it everything I need to let the power flow through me, manifesting my desire. The Higher Power IS supply; The Higher Power IS wealth, so there's nothing to fear... As The Higher Power is right where I am".

4. Grace: understand what you desire is yours. It's crucial to be thankful, because it acknowledges already having gotten the thing you want. The Higher Power doesn't need your gratitude, but to be fully aligned with the laws of the universe, you must feel the feeling of gratitude. This is the "already having gotten" attitude which adds fuel to the fire of your affirmative prayer. Therefore, you must understand how you'd feel if you had what you wish today.

5. Relinquish: and so, it is. Relinquishing is an essential step. When you're done, your brain ought to be at peace, clear, fearless, and watchful for signs of your desire showing up without getting obsessive about it! Allow the Law to work through you and make your desire a physical truth!

CHAPTER III

Intro To Cosmic Ordering

Synopsis

Cosmic Ordering isn't a fresh idea.

All religions give us this seed of wisdom – 'ask and you shall receive, seek and you shall find.'

Does it matter why it works? Don't let that stop you! What have you got to lose? In all ancient cultures the founding to become an excellent Magician involved embracing the understanding that the power of magic lies in the obvious. It's the simple things which produce miracles.

The Fundamentals

Your cosmic order will only be accomplished if you really feel you deserve it. The adage that if you don't love yourself how may anybody else love you is right. Love yourself and trust you deserve it, and the universe ought to put your order at the top.

A central point to remember is that we'll only get 'what we trust is conceivable' if you don't trust your order is possible, it has less chance of occurring. To trust you'll sprout wings and fly is course not going to occur, as your inner consciousness won't believe it's possible. Some individuals could never believe they'll win the lottery yet do it every week without fail. Someplace inside them there's a block and therefore it will never become truth.

My belief is that if you trust you deserve it and, crucially, believe it's conceivable, then it may happen. But it's crucial to listen to your inner guide. There's no point in ordering things you don't trust may happen as, by centering on your orders not happening, you're in effect wiping out your order!

So, begin by ordering things you do think may happen and, when you get the hang of it, aim higher.

The law of attraction – like draws in like. If you could change your frequency, you could change your life. Why is it that we duplicate patterns and draw the same sort of friends or lovers? Some individuals think that we give out a vibration that magnetically draws in others on a like vibration.

Our vibration is neutral – it doesn't understand what is good or bad for us so if we believe all men are traitorous, all jobs lead nowhere or we'll constantly be poor, we may attract those experiences. The media is forever flooding us with fear and bad news altogether out of proportion to reality. How may we make a shift to get our minds to trust in the positive?

Consciously practice being non-judgmental and compassionate. Be cognizant of your inner dialogue. If somebody succeeds or wins what is your response? Embrace the uniqueness in other people and viewpoints. Don't take things personally.

It's crucial to be aware of the energy you put out, as it is like a calling signal or lighthouse drawing in the same vibration back. If you get jealous or mad, if you're petty or judgmental, it's likely that you'll call in others who mimic this energy. We frequently have different rules for ourselves than other people.

If you've managed to embrace step one and two and know that you're worth it and believe that it's possible and go to the next step.

The world is your oyster so it's crucial to discover what it is you really want as that other old cliché 'be careful what you ask for' has never been more relevant!

Being in nature is an excellent way of becoming clear about your desires. In the stillness of nature, whenever I walk, is when I get my best ideas. Practice and enjoy knowing your ability to cosmically order grows with each success.

CHAPTER IV

Intro To Creative Visualization

Synopsis

Creative visualization is the procedure of utilizing your imagination in an integrated way, with the goal of producing what you wish in your life.

Seeing it

The procedure for visualization is simple:

Get relaxed; make use off your imagination to produce compelling images, sounds and feelings of you getting what you wish; Repeat!

If you continue centered on your target regularly - adding firm emotion - you'll be surprised to see your goals "turn up" in your life - frequently by unexplainable coincidences, or simply by gradual betterments.

The better you get at visualizing, the quicker you'll begin producing the life you wish.

Creative visualization is basically a technique to help you produce what you truly wish - whether that's more love, peace, fulfillment, self-expression, cash... Or anything else!

On the surface, it's great to get more of the things you wish. Without doubt. However, visualization goes deeper than that, much deeper!

Essentially, effective visualization involves exploring - and shifting - your deepest attitudes to life. This may have a fundamental effect on you!

You may become happier, more relaxed, more centered, mentally solider, more peaceful... and a whole lot more.

So, concisely, the answer to "why visualize?" is: because you'll get more of what you wish, but you'll likewise feel more favorable about life in general.

As Einstein wisely understood, "Your imagination is your preview of life's coming attractions". And originative visualization makes sure that the coming attractions are of your selecting!

The best way to begin visualization is to spend a couple of minutes before you go to bed, or just after you wake up, imagining - in as much detail as you may muster - what you wish in your life.

The secret key to visualization success is to bring forth the same favorable emotions you'd get if your dreams had already been achieved!

The more favorable emotions you feel, the quicker you'll influence your subconscious... and that's if you begin seeing results!

CHAPTER V

Intro To Mantras

Synopsis

So, you would like to get into mantra chanting. You're in luck—you can't get it wrong. Mantra chanting isn't the same thing as singing. You don't have to be perfect; you simply must want to open your heart in meditative peace and let your spirit spill out.

Connecting

There are a few matters to know about chanting as you start. There are 2 languages for chants sung in the Indian tradition: Sanskrit and Gurmukhi. Sanskrit is the language of Hindu chanting and is utilized by most yogic traditions except Kundalini Yoga, which is taken from the Sikh tradition and has chanting sung in the Gurmukhi language.

Chanting commonly involves repeating a mantra or a prayer. "Man" means mind and "tra" means across, so a mantra is something that's repeatedly crossing your brain to control your thoughts for meditation.

You're giving your hyperactive brain something holy to play with so that it calms. You can likewise interpret the word to mean a phrase which helps you to cross over your mind to get to your heart.

The words of a mantra are a vessel that takes you across the sea of your mind to arrive at the lands of the divine.

Repeating these words aloud has a particular effect on the body. As you state the mantra, your tongue is hitting meridian points on the top of the upper palate of the mouth, which impacts the energies going to other glands like the hypothalamus, the pineal, and the pituitary.

By arousing these meridian points, you're physically producing the effect of relaxation and a modified state of consciousness.

When you first begin, don't worry about your pronunciation and don't fret about hitting the correct notes. All of this will come with time. Chanting involves so much repeating, that you pick things up sooner or later.

It may be useful to look up the words of the mantra, because some of the times the sounds are so foreign to the average westerner that your brain gets a bit confused.

However, do not become caught up in perfection as you're starting out… All sounds made to the divine are great sounds.

The most crucial thing in chanting is your heart. Open it up wide. Ride the sound current like a wave. Feel the infinite divine right here, right now, within of you.

CHAPTER VI

Achieving A Positive Mindset

Being Positive

You're confirming in your mind something that you trust may be accomplished and by doing this it will become a fact. By utilizing favorable affirmations your subconscious will develop whatsoever favorable words are stated. Beginning every day correctly utilizing positive affirmations will affect the way you feel as well as the way youthink.

Positive affirmations will bring to life your capability to accomplish success.

Remember to continue repeating the statement (whatever you really believe you can attain) and block out all that damaging thinking. When you begin thinking of something negative, turn itaround into a positive.

Simply think of something completely different when those damaging thoughts arrive, you must always keep your thinking positive. This is how you utilize positive affirmations correctly.

Get in the correct mindset, grin, laugh, become that successful individual in your mind. Utilize those powerful favorable affirmations to tell your mind what you will do, then your subconscious will impactyour positive state.

Positive self-talk (Positive Affirmations) done repeatedly will drive you to an elevated standard of personal growth.

These are powerful statements that you are now able to use during your self-talk. You'll need to begin thinking as they have already occurred in your life. This is a vital factor, think like this is something that has already happened in the present, now, not tomorrow, next week or next month, now.

Do you really know what you want? You must figure this out, whether it's your goal, your ambitions, or even a wish. These positive affirmations must come directly from you and not anybody else to get to be effective.

You must be clear about the actions you're going to take, (whatsoever you tell yourself that you are able to and will do) then begin taking action toward achieving this goal. Don't let any negativity get in your way, remember repeat those positive affirmations whenever possible, as many as possible for as long as it takes. If you don't have a direction to take, you'll get confused and never become successful.

Remember what you think you'll produce! Utilize positive affirmations to produce your future beginning now!

Look… if you're struggling, I've been there …and I can tell you firsthand that it'll get better if you keep on trying.

CHAPTER VI

Writing Affirmations

Synopsis

Positive affirmations are simply a self-talk. This will help you reach whatsoever goals you have set for yourself. They may switch your thoughts, resulting from that negative self-talk to those more powerful positive thoughts.

Being Positive

While at first it might appear rather obvious, it may seem so unnecessary to include a chapter helping individuals to compose their own favorable affirmations. Having stated that, I do have suggestions that you might wish to consider if composing your own affirmations. Affirmations that are not only favorable in intent, but specifically and cautiously written by yourself with your events and problems in mind.

To effectively move your life positively and successfully forward, I suppose the most obvious place to start this rewarding exercise, would be to begin by listing and defining the precise reasons why you are wishing to compile and implement your own personalized affirmations in the first place.

Put differently, the issues, damaging thinking or problems that you are wishing to modify or improve can be dealt with by affirmations.

While it's much easier and simpler to utilize predefined affirmations generically written by somebody else, in all truthfulness, affirmations penned by the individual are typically more centered and mightier than their counterparts. I'm not of course discouraging you from utilizing prewritten affirmations, for they are incredibly useful, but experience suggests that more serious topics seem to react more favorably to more personalized and delicately tuned affirmations.

To help illustrate this point, I'll provide a fictitious example of a girl that we will name Emily, who experienced what she may only describe as bullying from one of her co-workers, who we'll name Joe, leaving Emily feeling more and more depressed, bitter and mad.

Along with other actions, Emily decided to introduce affirmations into her day-to-day routine, in the hope that these favorable statements would start to strengthen and increase her dropping confidence and inside strength.

Below are examples of the favorable affirmations that Emily thought about, the first is merely a prewritten affirmation as you may find at another source.

While the second affirmation was cautiously and mindfully written by herself. While both are appropriately useful, the second affirmation written by Emily, is more individualized and tailored towards her particular issue and problem, so understandably more effective.

I will not permit bullies to come into the sacred space of my soul.

Example of a personalized self-penned affirmation

I will not allow Joe to manipulate, bully or disrespect me. I'll remain calm, strong and resilient always.

As you may see, the self-written affirmation is more personalized, specifically mentioning Emily's bully by name, along with the fashion and way that Emily is wishing to react.

Two crucial tips that you might wish to think about when writing your own affirmations. However, simply a word of caution, while it might be tempting to write something damaging about the issues, individuals or issue causing your distress, Joe in Emily's example.

This would entirely alter the dynamic and purpose of what should be a favorable, self-empowering exercise into something ratherdamaging.

For while Emily mentioned Joe in our affirmation, Emily is merely self-affirming how she would personally like to respond and react, and not inferring harm or negativity toward Joe, this would be damaging and unloving.

CHAPTER VIII

Using Affirmations

Synopsis

Affirmations may help you to alter harmful behaviors or achieve goals, and they may likewise help undo the damage caused by damaging scripts, those things which we repeatedly tell ourselves (or which other people repeatedly tell us) that contribute to a damaging self-perception. Affirmations are simple to create and utilize, but you'll need dedication to make them work.

Doing It Right

Consider your positive attributes. Scrutinize of yourself by making an inventory of your best qualities, abilities, or other attributes. Are you gorgeous? Put it down. Are you a hard worker? Make note of it. Write every quality down in a short sentence, beginning with "I" and utilizing the present tense: "I am beautiful," for instance, or "I'mgenerous".

These statements are affirmations of who you are. We seldom center on those things that we truly like about ourselves, instead deciding to linger over things we'd like to change. An inventory will help you break that cycle and utilizing these affirmations to help you appreciate who you are will present you the confidence you need to accept your affirmations of who you wish to be.

Consider what damaging scripts you wish to counteract or what positive goals you wish to achieve. Affirmations may be highly useful to counteract damaging perceptions you have developed. Affirmations may likewise help you accomplish goals, like losing weight or stopping smoking. Make a list of your goals or the harmful self- perceptions you wish to alter.

Prioritize your list of things to work on. You might find that you have a lot of goals or that you need a lot of counter-scripts. It's best, however, to center simply a few affirmations at a time, so select those that are most crucial or most urgent and work with those first. Once you see betterment in those areas or achieve those goals you may develop new affirmations for additional items on your list.

Write your affirmations. Add other affirmations to influence your conduct in the future. The affirmations you'll utilize to influence future changes ought to follow the basic form. They should begin with "I," and be short, clear, and positive.

Match up some of your favorable attributes with your goals. Which of the favorable qualities that you affirmed earlier will help you accomplish the goals you have set? If you're stopping smoking, for instance, you might need willpower or courage, or you might need to reflect on the fact that you're pretty or that you care about your loved ones. Choose 2 or 3 of these affirmations to support your goal- oriented affirmations.

Make your affirmations visible so you may utilize them. Repeating is the key to making affirmations effective. You wish to think about your affirmations a lot of times a day, daily. There are numerous ways to do this.

Make a point of writing your affirmations in a journal or diary every morning when you get up and every night before you turn in. Repeat the affirmations to yourself at these times, as well. Ideally, your affirmations ought to be the first thing you think of when you get up and the last before you turn in.

Meditate on your affirmations. Shut your eyes, keep out the rest of the world, and consider your affirmations. Say and repeat the words but consider what the words mean to you; consider the future and try to feel the emotions that the affirmations bring up.

Leave reminder cards in assorted places. Utilize 3X5 index cards or sticky notes to write your affirmations (one per card). Make numerous cards for each affirmation, and then leave these cards where you'll see them: place one where you sit at the kitchen table, tape one to your automobile steering wheel, slip one inside your desk drawer, or stick one to your PC monitor, etc. Every time you see the card, read it and consider what it means.

Carry your affirmations with you. Create a list of your affirmations and put it in your billfold or purse. If you need a pick-me-up, or if you discover yourself about to waver from your goals, take out your affirmations and read them.

CHATER IX

Advantages And Disadvantages

Synopsis

Positive affirmation or positive self-talk may benefit not only yourself but likewise other individuals that you interact with. Affirmation is the switching of thoughts resulting from damaging, dirty, and rough experiences or ideas to a more positive note. It relies on the principle that you may only become successful if you tell yourself "I can do that" rather than saying, "I can't do that."

The Good and the Bad

If you believe that positive affirmation impacts only the subconscious, then wait till you hear this. Studies have determined that individuals who perpetually bombard themselves with positive words instead of entertaining damaging thoughts and words have more substantialmuscles.

Research claims that an individual's muscles get stronger and more active when the subconscious mind is filled with favorable words. The same report indicated that the human muscles tend to get weak when an individual thinks and verbalizes that he's tired or that he hates the world or that he can't do a certain thing.

Aside from muscle strength, positive affirmation likewise impacts your energy level. A happy individual is commonly a result of a positive mind programming.

Positive affirmation does not only affect the physical but likewise the emotional well-being of an individual. Because of this, experts have always advised individuals to start their day with good and positive thoughts and words.

Starting the day right would extend the vibrant feeling throughout the day and would even act as a multiplier effect to all other positive aspects in your life.

Positive affirmation brings to life an individual's capabilities, strengths, talents, and skills. Perpetually repeating the things that you're capable of doing and forgetting hesitant feelings that commonly hinder you from going after a certain goal may help a lot inaccomplishing a positive result.

A light outlook, a smiling face, and a worry-free aura are commonly the features of very successful individuals. The principle of positive affirmation leans on the core tenets that the mind is just so mighty and what it says is commonly followed and miraculously accomplished by the body.

Our thoughts, self-talk and affirmations, both positive and negative, get to be self-fulfilling prophesies much more often than not. Your actions and effort are influenced by what you're thinking, so if you think you'll fail at something you likely will. Likewise, if you think you'll succeed you likely will.

Most individuals don't realize that it is possible to choose to more think more positively. The consequences of such a choice are that your consequences are truly the ones you consciously want.

For instance, if you're attempting to slim down...

DON'T say or think, "I'm not going to cheat on my diet, and I'll lose weight no matter what."

The above supposedly positive thinking affirmation might lead to the person becoming dangerously skinny and/or under nourished. By saying "no matter what" in the affirmation, the individual could end up overdoing things. They could make them self seriously ill in their quest to slim down, although this was never the intent.

So, it's crucial to think things through and avoid producing unwanted side effects when composing your affirmations. With the above dieting affirmation, quite apart from the words "no matter what" making it potentially harmful, it uses the wrong tense. It might be further improved by selecting more meaningful positive words.

CHAPTER X

Conclusion

Make use of *POSTIVE WORDS* in your affirmation instead of utilizing words which serve to remind you of something you wish to eradicate. Producing the affirmation in the positive is much more effective.

DON'T say and think, "I'm not shy" or "I'm not insecure"

Rather SAY and THINK, "I'm outgoing" or "I'm secure" or "I'm confident"

When writing an affirmation, ask yourself what is it that you fundamentally want. Then compose the affirmation based on your answer to this question, instead of focusing and constructing your affirmation on what you don't want.

Again, your actions and effort are influenced by your thinking, self-talk and affirmations. Centering on being outgoing, secure and confident is much more likely to bring about the results you want, than using an affirmation which veers toward what you're trying to overcome (in that instance avoid the words "shy" and "insecure").

A different example - if you want to feel confident about making a speech you put up SAY and THINK "I'm a confident and articulate public speaker" instead of saying "I'm not anxious about public speaking and I don't falter over my words". In that instance, steer clear of framing your affirmation in the negative by quashing the words "anxious" and "falter".

The power of positive affirmations is amazing when you cautiously frame your affirmations in a manner which doesn't inadvertently create unwanted results.

When you utilize the present tense, positive meaningful words and aim high in a reasonable, realistic and incremental manner as described in this book, challenges which have defeated you in the past can be effectively tackled. If you wish to enhance your life, it's time to decide to think positively.

www.ingramcontent.com/pod-product-compliance
Lightning Source LLC
LaVergne TN
LVHW091243150826
845673LV00003B/1265

* 9 7 9 8 3 5 1 6 1 1 1 5 0 *